Denmark

Denmark is a land of gentle plains and low, rolling hills. Almost every bit of the country is used for growing crops or for grazing animals. The efficient and highly productive agricultural system produces more than the Danes require. Consequently, Denmark is one of the few advanced nations to have a high level of agricultural exports. Two-thirds of these go to the EEC (European Economic Community, or "Common Market").

In the last twenty years there has been an increase in investment in manufacturing industry. This is now a thriving, export-oriented sector of the economy – a surprising fact when you realize that Denmark lacks any raw materials or natural sources of energy.

Now this small island community of 5 million inhabitants has one of the highest standards of living and social welfare in the whole of Europe.

The Danes like to think of themselves as intelligent, well-educated, industrious, and artistically gifted people. By reading this book, you will find that their opinion of themselves is well founded.

Ulla Andersen has travelled extensively around her homeland in the course of writing this book.

SKAGERRAK

SWEDEN

Skagen

Hjørring

Lindholm

Ålborg

KATTEGAT

Rold Forest

Struer

Holstebro

Ikast

Århus

Elsinore

Frederikssund

Farum

NORTH SEA

JUTLAND

Roskilde

Copenh

ZEALAND

Esbjerg

Jullerup

Hasmark

Lumby

Odense

Køge

Slagelse

Rødding

Baagø

FUNEN

Assens

Fakse

WEST GERMANY

EAST GERM

we live in
DENMARK

Ulla Andersen

A Living Here Book

The Bookwright Press
New York · 1984

Living Here

First published in the United States in 1984 by
The Bookwright Press, 387 Park Avenue South,
New York NY 10016

First published in 1982 by
Wayland (Publishers) Limited, England.

© Copyright 1982 Wayland (Publishers) Ltd.
All rights reserved

ISBN: 0–531–04782–2

Library of Congress Catalog Card Number: 83–72804

Printed by G. Canale & C.S.p.A., Turin, Italy

Contents

"Most of these newspapers are regional"

Birger Christensen is 46 and a journalist on a regional paper, the *Frederiksborg Amtsavis*. He is also very interested in local television broadcasting and recently visited Japan to see how their local TV stations operate.

There are 48 daily newspapers published in Denmark, and the overall circulation is about 1.4 million. This seems like a lot when you consider that the total population of Denmark is only around 5 million; but I suppose it works out at about one per household per day. Most of these papers are regional, like the one that I work for, and are published in the morning. Most people know what is going on in the big

Birger's job is to supply the Frederiksborg Amtsavis *with material on Frederikssund.*

wide world from the radio or TV, so the regional papers can concentrate on local affairs and cultural matters. The two main national papers, *Ekstra Bladet* and *Berlingske Tidende*, are published in the capital, Copenhagen, in the morning.

When I first started as a journalist, in the mid-fifties, there were a lot more papers than there are today. Most of them were mouthpieces for a particular political party: there was a Conservative paper, a Social-Liberal paper, a Social Democrat paper and a Liberal paper. Nowadays, the reporting in most papers is more politically neutral. But, of course, some papers still have a certain point of view on everything: *Land og Folk* is a Communist paper, and *Aktuelt* supports the Social Democrats. No Danish newspaper, though, is directly controlled by the State. Most of them are in the hands of individuals, companies or trusts.

The *Frederiksborg Amtsavis* is, I suppose, a Liberal paper; but that doesn't matter much in our day-to-day treatment of

the news. Most of the articles we feature are about everyday life in the local communities throughout the region of north Sjaelland.

The Christensen family always take part in Frederikssund's annual play about Vikings, which lasts seventeen days!

People in Denmark don't only get their news from a newspaper, or course. At the moment we have only one television channel. This is run by the central broadcasting institution, *Danmarks Radio*. *Danmarks Radio* is publicly owned, but run by an independent council of twenty-seven members, who are chosen by Parliament. All broadcasting is financed by licenses which are bought by TV owners.

Neither the TV nor the radio channels carry any advertising, although it is possible that there may soon be another, commercial, TV channel. Danish TV and radio carry only a few foreign language broadcasts. There is only one language spoken throughout the whole of Denmark, and so nearly all broadcasting is in Danish; although there are news summaries in English, German, French and Eskimo. Many of our TV programs are from abroad, with Danish subtitles.

A future TV project that I'm very interested in is local TV stations, carrying similar news and features to those in the *Frederiksborg Amtsavis*. These local stations are already being set up on a trial basis in a number of regions. The idea is for organizations and people from the local communities to provide the material for broadcasting; professionals may be involved at some later date.

I recently visited Japan to see how their local TV stations operate and came back with some interesting ideas which I hope I can put into practice to make local TV work here as well.

"We have a good welfare system in Denmark"

Kasper Kaarøe is 29. A lithographer by trade, he is currently unemployed and attending one of Denmark's ninety folk high schools while he is waiting for a job.

It's a bit difficult to explain exactly what a folk high school is, but I'll try. As a people, we Danes are very eager to learn and to discover things about the country we live in, particularly those things which are not taught to us in normal high schools. So we have folk high schools. These are boarding schools which can be attended by men and

Kasper has been studying at Rødding Folk High School for four months.

women of any age. There are ninety folk high schools around the country, and about 10,000 people go to them. No two folk schools are the same, either in appearance or in the kind of courses they offer. Very often the schools are in old manor houses or castles, but we also have a number of quite new ones.

Many of the schools are based upon the ideas of the nineteenth-century poet and priest, Nikolai Grundtvig, who wanted to improve the education of farmers' children so that they could live better lives. The main focus used to be on Christianity and cultural subjects, but the schools have kept pace with the times. At Rødding, we're currently doing experiments into alternative sources of energy. I'm studying ceramics, religion, ecological farming, Danish and the social sciences. We have to study for twenty-eight hours a week; on top of which there may be evening lectures. There are no exams at the end, which is quite a relief! It's nice just to be learning for its own sake.

Ninety per cent of the students here are

unemployed. They're either between jobs or trying to get an apprenticeship. Unemployment is a major problem in Denmark, just as it is in other countries around the world. At the moment, about twelve per cent of the total labor force is without work. But we have a good welfare system in Denmark. The State pays for the running of schools like this through subsidies, and unemployment insurance pays you ninety per cent of what you would be earning if you were employed.

I'm waiting for a job as a production assistant with an advertising agency. I'm a lithographer (lithography is a printing process) by trade. I had four years' training, plus two years at a school for graphic design. It's very frustrating not being able to find a job after all the training I went through, but at least with folk high schools I don't have to spend my time twiddling my thumbs at home.

Even when I have finished here and, I hope, got a job, I might decide to continue my education in one of our night schools. We have an extensive night-school system for adults in Denmark. Every town has its night school, and over 600,000 people a year go to evening classes. They pay part of the fees themselves, and the local council pays the rest. And they go solely because they want to learn a bit more.

Kasper is learning pottery – one of the many crafts taught at Rødding Folk High School.

"The State looks after old people"

Marie Hansine Schmidt, 88, and her husband, Hilmar, live in Jullerup, on the island of Fyn. Hilmar is a retired village postman. They have just celebrated sixty-five years of marriage, and received a congratulatory letter from the Queen of Denmark.

I wasn't really looking forward to Hilmar's retirement. I thought it would make our lives very difficult. But, in Denmark, the State looks after old people, and the last twenty years or so have not really been a hardship at all.

We both get old-age pensions and have since Hilmar was 67. They are paid for out of government funds from the taxes that we have paid throughout our lives.

Marie Hansine always enjoys a game of cards when her grandchildren come to visit her.

About fifty per cent of all the money that Danes earn goes for taxes. We still pay taxes now, but that's because we've saved up so much money, and we have to pay tax on the interest that we get from our savings. If we didn't have any savings the State would give us even more assistance, such as a rent subsidy, free telephone, and assistance in the home for cleaning and cooking.

Because of the unemployment situation here in Denmark, the State is trying to get people to retire early. People aged 60 or over can leave work and get what's called an "after-wage" – a wage equal to unemployment benefit (about ninety per cent of the wage they would have earned if they had continued working). This is a good thing, I suppose, because it means that there are more jobs available to the young people who need them most.

I can't do very much these days after breaking my arm once and my thighbone twice. Luckily, we have a free health service. Hospitals and medical centers are all paid for by the State, but are

Marie Hansine's husband, Hilmar, looks after the garden of their house in Jullerup.

run by local authorities. I wear a hearing aid and glasses, which are provided by the local authority. They even pay for a car to take me to the medical center in Odense!

The State tries to help old people so that they can live in their own homes for as long as possible. A few of the old people we know, though, have gone into nursing homes and apartments for the elderly. They can live there independently, but they have a bell so that they can always ring for a nurse. That way they're always safe. If you live in a nursing home, though, almost all of your pension goes toward paying the fees. Hilmar and I would rather stay here at home; not that there's much for us to spend money on at our age.

Our children, grandchildren and great-grandchildren often come to visit us. We like to set out a good meal for them; real Danish food like roast pork and *mettwurst* (a kind of sausage made of minced pork), with potatoes, gravy and pickled cucumber. Most of the vegetables come from our own little garden, which Hilmar looks after.

We've just celebrated our sixty-fifth wedding anniversary and we got a letter from Queen Margrethe II. When we celebrate a wedding anniversary in this country — a silver wedding anniversary (twenty-five years) or a golden wedding anniversary (fifty years) — the neighbors and children decorate the door to your home with branches. It's an old tradition in country villages. It looks so festive, and the whole neighborhood can see that you're celebrating. In the old days we'd have a party in the village hall and invite maybe fifty or a hundred people. We're a bit too old for that sort of thing now though!

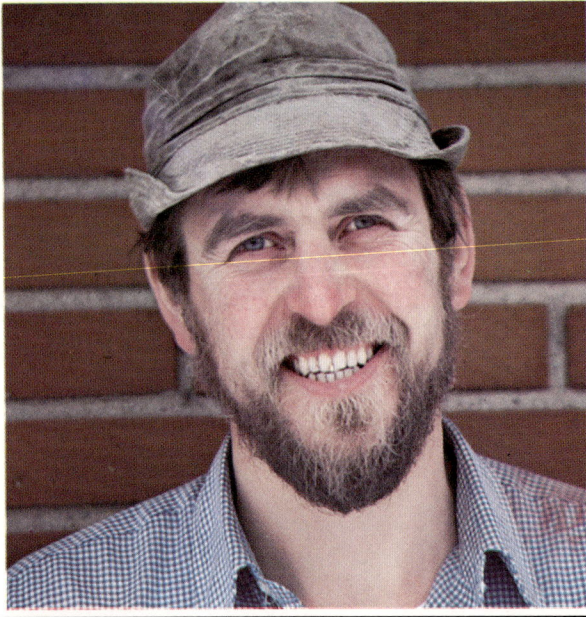

"Farming has to be in your blood"

Knud Sørensen, age 37, is a farmer in the west of Sjaelland island. Besides raising pigs, from which Danish bacon is made, he grows barley and sugar beets on this 27-hectare (68-acre) farm.

Raising pigs is so important to the Danish economy that there are roughly twice as many pigs as Danes in Denmark. On my farm we have about 900 to 1,000 pigs in the stalls at any one time. About 70 of these are one-year-old sows – we call them *gilts* – and they produce 1,200 pigs for slaughter each year. The pigs are sent to the slaughterhouse in Slagelse. As with most Danish slaughterhouses, this is co-operatively owned; about 5,000 farmers have shares in it. In fact, the world's first agricultural cooperative was founded in Denmark, in 1882. We now have thousands of co-operatively owned dairies, bacon-curing factories, and egg-packing plants.

Although the cooperatives make farming more efficient, these days it isn't easy

Knud feeding some of his 1,000 pigs. In Denmark, pigs outnumber humans by 2 to 1!

being a farmer. A small farmer with a mixed stock just can't make ends meet. You have to do everything on a large scale if you want to show any kind of profit. But if you borrow money to invest in a whole lot of new machinery, you still have problems because the interest rates are so high. You have to find a balance between your investments and your returns. True enough, we do get subsidies from the State to help with the interest repayments, but it seems to me that the proper thing to do would be for the farmers to get high enough prices to enable them to manage for themselves.

Farmers don't have a trade union as such. We do belong to a National Union of Farmers, which looks after our interests. But the minute we wanted to strike, we wouldn't get any financial help. And, besides, we don't want to see food thrown away — which is what would happen if we went on strike. But it would be nice if farmers could stick up for themselves a bit more. That way perhaps we would get better working conditions.

Only about 7 per cent of the working population is employed in agriculture, and we could certainly use more people. I suppose people are discouraged because the wages are too low. Also farming isn't something that you can just pick up as you go along. It really has to be in your blood. My father taught me to start with, and later I took a number of different agricultural courses. I still keep up-to-date by going to courses each winter, which are arranged by the National Union of Farmers. The young farmers today go to agricultural college for six to nine months, and after that they do some practical training on a farm.

The farm we're living on dates back to 1875 but it's been in the family for only about 30 years. I took it over from my father. We have 27 hectares (68 acres) of land. We use four-fifths for growing barley and one-fifth for sugar beets. We use the barley for pig feed and send the beets to a sugar refinery. Our barley only makes up a third of the pig feed we need, and we have to buy the rest. Of all the costs involved in pig raising, 80 per cent goes on feed. A pig needs feeding for seven months before it's ready for slaughtering. It can eat a lot of food in that time!

The pigs themselves have been specially bred over the last 70 years to have less fat and larger hams. Danish pigs are longer in the body because they actually have two more ribs than other breeds. Much of the meat is exported — generally speaking you could say that the British eat our bacon, the Americans eat our canned ham, and we ourselves eat pork sausages and roasts.

I'm what you might call a "traditional" Danish farmer, but there is a new movement in farming — ecological farming — which doesn't use chemical foodstuffs or fertilizers. I don't think it will catch on though. Some farmers might be able to supply specialist health shops, but the ordinary consumer won't like the higher prices that result from growing without artificial fertilizer.

In winter, the fields of Knud's farm are often hidden beneath a thick layer of snow.

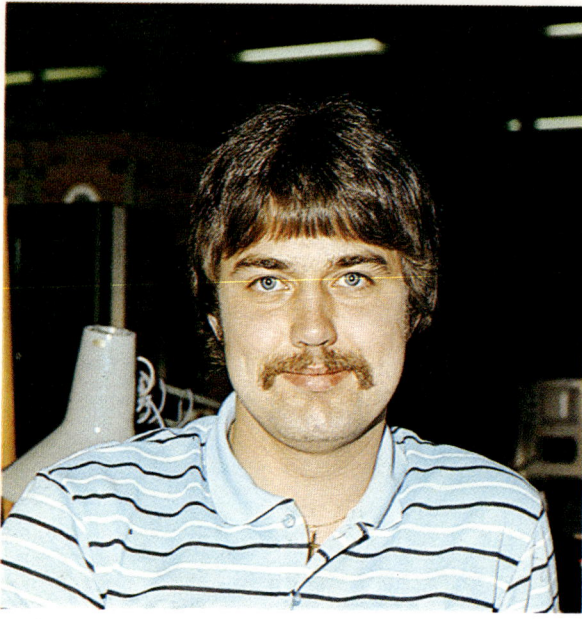

"Denmark has few natural resources"

John Børge Jensen is 27 and lives in Holstebro. He works for the famous electronics firm, Bang and Olufsen, in Struer, some 15 km (9 miles) from his home.

Bang and Olufsen televisions, radios, hi-fi equipment and accessories are famous throughout the world. From the point of view of quality, there aren't many who can touch us; but then we do spend a lot of energy and money developing products which will last for many years.

It's encouraging for the company's workers to see the firm doing so well,

John tests the printed circuits of television sets to see that they work properly.

especially as a large part of our sales are in the export market. About seventy-five per cent of all the goods we produce are sold overseas – and that's in spite of the fact that they are more expensive than many of our competitors' products.

Most firms in Denmark are dependent upon exports for their survival. This is because Denmark has few natural resources. We have made a number of discoveries of oil and natural gas recently, but these are not productive yet. All of our coal, steel, tin, lead, and cotton must be imported, and we must pay for these imports from the sale of our agricultural and manufactured products. In fact, Denmark has one of the highest levels of foreign trade per inhabitant in the whole world.

Here in Struer, one in every three families is connected with the Bang and Olufsen company. The town has 15,000 inhabitants, so it goes without saying that the firm means a lot to the town. In Danish terms, this is a big organization; 3,000 people are employed in this factory (the

national average is about sixty employees per company). In terms of turnover, we are in the top one hundred companies in the country, with an annual turnover of over one billion kroner ($100 million). Like most of Danish industry, Bang and Olufsen is privately owned and run, and we get no subsidies from the State.

The company also has subsidiaries in other countries – ten in all. The newest one is in Japan, and we feel that this is a real feather in our cap, especially when you think of how fierce the competition is between Japanese products and ours – even though Bang and Olufsen products are in quite a different price bracket in the foreign markets.

The wages here aren't terribly high, but it's a really good place to work. I've just been offered another job, where I'd get 10 kroner ($1.00) more per hour; but I turned it down because everyone gets along so well here. About half of all I earn is paid over to the State in the form of taxes. This might seem like a lot, but I suppose someone has to pay for the welfare state and for the maintenance of our roads, harbors and railroads.

Every morning I drive up here from my home in Holstebro. I share the expense with several other workers because there isn't much in the way of public transportation here. My wife is out of work at the moment, so she stays at home and looks after our son. I don't think that I'll be thrown out of work in the near future though. Electronics is one of the big growth industries at the moment. With the machinery and measuring instruments industries, it forms the metal-processing industry, which has one of the highest export ratings in the country. I just hope that Bang and Olufsen can stay on top.

"Burial mounds are a feature of the countryside"

Merete Harding, 24, is a history student in her fifth year at Copenhagen University. To help pay for her studies, she teaches children four hours a week at the Viking Ship Museum in Roskilde.

I left school at 18 and started working toward my history degree. I'm in the fifth year at Copenhagen University now, but I'm figuring on staying for another three or four years. This probably seems like a lot, but many students in Denmark stay at the university for up to ten years.

There are only five universities in Denmark, three technical universities and many centers that specialize in the teaching of certain subjects. Entry is limited to about 20,000 places every year. So although, in theory, everyone has a chance to go to college, in practice, admission is restricted. You've got to have very good school qualifications, and maybe some work experience before you can get in.

Aside from the entry restrictions, there is the problem of paying for studies. Although education at all levels is provided free by the State, students still have to find money to live on, and few parents can afford to maintain their children at college for the length of time that it takes to get a degree. You can get a grant of about 18,000 kroner ($1800) a year from the Young People's Education Fund, but it's not really enough to live on. Students can also borrow money from the State — around 30,000 kroner ($3000) a year — which you don't have to pay back until you have finished your studies. But there are so many rules about getting a grant like this that many students don't apply for them.

Almost every student in Denmark, therefore, has to have a job while they are studying. I am lucky enough to be able to do four hours' teaching a week at the Viking Ship Museum at Roskilde, about 16 km (10 miles) away. The museum allows schools to visit for lessons and use our facilities. It's a very vivid form of history teaching. We've got five Viking ships in the exhibition hall, and the children and I can go around and look at them together.

The Viking period is one of the most exciting in the history of Denmark and lasted from about A.D. 800 to 1000. You can still find traces of the Vikings all over Denmark. We have a number of forts, such

The museum at Roskilde, where Merete works part-time, has five Viking ships on display.

as those at Trelleborg, Aggersborg and Fyrkat, and boat graves, like the enormous one at Lindholm, which has 700 graves gathered in one spot. But the history of Denmark goes back further than the Vikings. Bronze Age people built large barrows (burial mounds for their dead), and these still form a characteristic feature of the Danish countryside.

Copenhagen is the capital of Denmark and also the largest city in the country. It's a great place to live and is also very beautiful. Its lovely spires and towers have earned it the name "the city of beautiful spires." Copenhagen is the center for cultural activities, too, and the Royal Theater is the largest theater in the country.

The Viking graveyard at Lindholm, near Alborg, has some 700 graves all about 1000 years old.

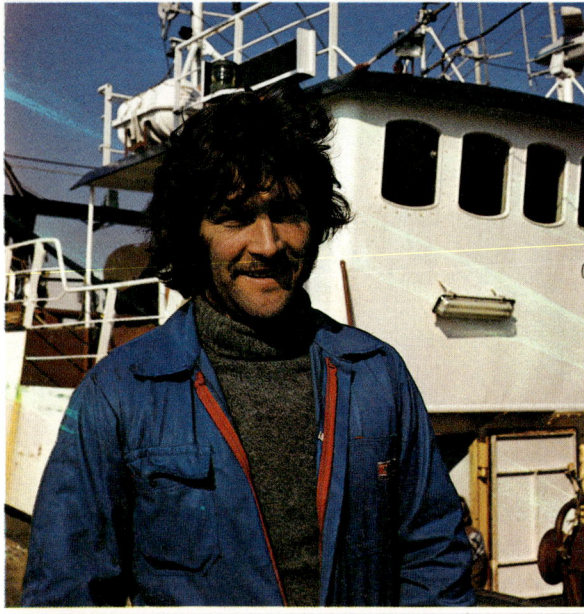

"There are fewer and fewer of us fishermen left"

John Allan Hansen is 31 and the skipper of a trawler, based in Esbjerg, Denmark's biggest fishing port. He and his crew of three fish the Dogger Bank in the North Sea. In winter, the water there is so cold that falling overboard can be fatal.

My ship's a trawler. Many Danish fishing vessels are made of wood, but mine's iron, and it has one trawl. The holds can carry up to 242 tons of fish. We have to keep fishing until the holds are full, and that can take ten days or more, sometimes. Costs and overheads are so high these days that only a full load makes the trip worthwhile. The huge price increases in oil over the

The trawler's crew unloading part of a large catch of cod from the North Sea.

past six years have made a big difference to our running costs, especially as a ship this size can use about 10,000 liters (2,200 gallons) of fuel in a week.

We catch mainly what we call "trash" fish, that's to say fish for industrial purposes – used for processing into fishmeal, fish oil and food for the mink farms. The most important of these fish is the sand eel, and apart from that we catch herring and whatever else we come across. In the old days the whole catch went to the fishmeal factory, but now we sort it out, so that any fish for human consumption can be sold separately at the early-morning auctions at Esbjerg. The prices for these fish are much higher than for industrial fish.

We share the profit from each catch. Fifty per cent goes for fueling the ship and maintaining the equipment, and the rest is divided among us. I get the largest share, and the amount the others get depends on how long they've been working for me. All Danish fishing boats work like this.

Out of a working population of about 1.3 million, only 11,000 men in Denmark earn their living from fishing. Our ships caught about 2 million tons of salt-water fish in 1976, but the amount has gone down a bit since then. Even so, Denmark is still the second largest fishing nation in Europe.

Here in Denmark we eat mainly plaice, cod and herring. One fish that we relish is the eel, which we can catch in lakes or salt water. We eat it in the summer with boiled potatoes. And, of course, we have to have a beer and a glass of aquavit (liquor made from grain or potatoes, flavored with spices) to wash it down with – we say the eel has got to "swim" down to your stomach!

There are now a number of EEC regulations about how many fish we're allowed to catch, and the deep trawl nets are forbidden. When we've caught our quota, we're not allowed to catch any more. I think it's wrong and the marine biologists should listen more to the fishermen. After all, we're "on the spot" and can judge whether the fish are disappearing in any numbers.

Some of what they say is true; if there were only small fry (baby fish) then we wouldn't put the nets out anyhow. And in some respects the EEC has done some good by allowing our ships into other waters to fish, so we're not restricted to just the waters off Denmark. But there are still some areas in the Baltic and off Norway and Sweden that we can't use.

We've been fishing for many years, and there's still plenty of fish in the sea – there always will be – although you could argue that our methods of catching them are becoming more sophisticated all the time. But I'm sure that these quota arrangements must be partly to blame for the fact that so many of the smaller fishermen have had to sell their boats. There are fewer and fewer of us fishermen left, and fewer of the large fishing boats too.

This trailer-load of "trash" fish will be used for animal food, oil and fishmeal.

"The Danes love children"

Kurt Dirchsen, 36, has been a teacher at the Drosselbro day care center for a year. The center is situated in Brøndby Strand, a modern suburb of the Danish capital, Copenhagen.

I'm in charge of fifteen children, aged from two to four. Day care centers for young Danish children are divided by age into three groups: day nurseries take children up to the age of three; kindergartens take children aged three to six; and youth centers take children aged six to twelve. Drosselbro is one of a new type of day care center, which cater to children from the ages of two to twelve. At the moment we have about fifty-two children here.

Kurt has been a kindergarten teacher at the Drosselbro center for a year now.

The Brøndby Strand housing complex in a suburb of Copenhagen has 10,000 inhabitants.

In Denmark, children must start school at the age of seven and must have at least nine years of schooling. Education is free from the age of seven, but parents must pay to send their children to day care institutions.

If parents have a low income, they can get a subsidy from their local authority to support sending their children to a day care center. This applies particularly to one-parent families. There are quite a few single mothers and fathers with children in the Brøndby Strand area. Besides being eligible for subsidies, they also go to the top of the waiting list when it comes to allocating places in the centers – because, after all, they're the only breadwinner in the family, and if they could not work they would have to rely on the State to support them.

The Brøndby Strand is quite a new housing development of about 10,000 inhabitants living in 3,000 apartments. In this part of the city, as in the rest of Denmark, I suppose, it's quite common now for both parents to work, so they need someone to look after their children for the day. Many of the people in this area work in the center of Copenhagen, which means that they spend a lot of time commuting, and are often not back home until quite late. Some of our pupils are here from 7 a.m. until 5 p.m. That's a long day when you're only two! But we do our best to keep them amused. We give breakfast to the children who arrive very early. At 9 o'clock we have morning assembly and call the roll. We also sing songs and talk about the time of year and what is going on in the world around us. We take them on field trips, study daily topics, and let them play until they are collected by their parents.

It may sound as if the Danish people do not care about their children, leaving them at places like this all day at a very early age, but this is not the case at all. The Danes love children. City planners always leave open spaces for parks and gardens when they are planning a new development, and by law all new apartment blocks must have special children's play spaces around them. Many Danish cities, including Copenhagen, have junk playgrounds: open spaces where children can use bricks, boxes, old planks and other bits of junk to build caves, castles or whatever else takes their fancy.

21

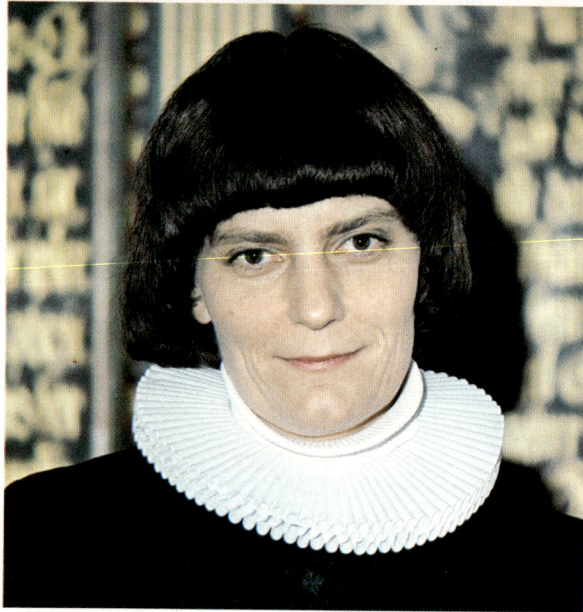

"There's more to life than cars and boats"

The Reverend Elisabeth Lyneborg, aged 42, is the Vicar of Farum, a suburb of Copenhagen. She became a priest six years ago and now leads a busy life looking after her parish and her five children. Yet she has had the time to write three books.

I enjoy being a priest, especially here in the suburbs. There are two churches in this parish: an old one dating back to the thirteenth century and a modern one built in 1981. I preach in both of them. The new church has also got a number of meeting rooms. There we have confirmation classes. Sunday school – well actually it's on Saturdays over here – for the younger children, and social get-togethers for the older children. At the moment I'm working on setting up a youth club: if we don't offer young people some Christian alternative, they end up turning to Oriental religions, where all they do is sit and meditate the whole time.

Christianity can really give people a meaning to life and, in my opinion, it's the only thing that can save the world from war and strife. The central theme of Christianity is love – really wanting the best for your fellow man. Because of this I think we are justified in carrying our missionary work to the far corners of the Earth. Otherwise other religions will only get in

there first, and it's my belief that Christianity is the best of them.

The Danish constitution provides for religious freedom, but about 94 per cent of the population belong to the Lutheran Church *(Folke Kirken)*, which is a branch of the Protestant faith. The largest non-Lutheran community in Denmark is the Roman Catholic Church.

Female clergy are looked upon as something rather extraordinary in many other countries. Here in Denmark they are becoming more or less accepted now. Actually 12 per cent of Denmark's clergy are women and many new ones are being ordained. But traditionally it's a man's profession, so you still get a certain amount of prejudice. Some religious groups still refuse to recognize female priests. I don't really understand exactly why some people are so afraid of having female priests. It must be the traditional distribution of sex roles.

It's a big job being a vicar today. For many years people have been wrapped up

Elisabeth tells her local scout troop about the youth club she is setting up.

with material possessions – keeping up with the Joneses. But the youth revolt of the 1960s did shake some of those ideas, and today many young people realize there's more to life than cars and boats.

Our job as people of the Church is to get the Christian message through to them. We can only do that by speaking their language. For that reason I cut out all the words in my sermons that might not be understood. If there is a special word which I do have to use, I explain it in the form of a story.

Whether or not you're accepted as a female vicar is really up to you. But women are often a bit more in touch with things than men – more down-to-earth. After all, they're mothers and housewives like other women, and often its easier to talk with a woman about your problems than it is with a man. So I think that there should be male and female priests in every parish.

The old church in Elisabeth's parish isn't always so empty when she preaches there!

23

"We're allowed to drink as much beer as we want"

Frede Bay Hansen is a worker at the Faxe brewery in Fakse. He is 61 years old, and soon to retire on an early-pension scheme, so that a younger person can take up his job.

This summer I'll be celebrating working here for forty years. That sounds like a long time, but it doesn't seem it. Perhaps it's because I enjoy my work or because I feel I've played my part in building up a successful business.

The brewery is a family concern, started in 1901 by Conrad Nielsen and his wife Nikoline. The brewery is still a family

Bottles line up, waiting to be filled with beer in the bottling plant at the brewery.

business, even though it is quoted on the stock exchange and some of the shares are owned by the nation. We have 8,000 shareholders, a number of whom work for the brewery.

It gives you a special relationship to your place of work when you're a part-owner. Of course, one share doesn't mean much in itself, but put together they give us workers quite a number of votes. We also have a great deal of influence in lots of other things. For example, I'm on the board of the company as one of the representatives of the employees. We have a law in Denmark which says that when a company employs more that fifty workers, there must be at least one workers' representative on the board.

We aren't as large as the three main breweries in Denmark – United Breweries, Carlsberg and Tuborg. But we are able to compete with them and, over the last ten years, we've won a good deal of the market from them.

We used to produce canned beer for our

home markets. But in 1981 the Ministry for the Environment banned its sale in Denmark, because cans, unlike bottles, cannot be re-used. So now we only export canned beer, to such countries as West Germany, Sweden, Belgium and a little to Britain. In all, about twenty per cent of our products are made for export.

Our sales of mineral waters are doing very well: we have 20 per cent of the total Danish market, whereas Tuborg and Carlsberg only have 17 per cent each. But then we have the world's best water here, Fakse is situated on a chalk bed. The whole subsoil consists of chalk, and the water we pump up is particularly good. We have about a dozen wells from which we pump up water for our production.

This summer I'll be stopping work and taking early retirement. This means that I will receive a lump sum from the firm and then be paid the same as unemployment benefit, which corresponds to 90 per cent of what I earn now. After two years, it goes down to 80 per cent; then after another two years down to 60 per cent until you get to the normal retirement age at 67. A lot of people have decided to retire early so that young people can take over their jobs.

It has been worked out that every year a Dane drinks 153 liters (268 pints) of beer on average, which is quite a lot when you think that there are some people who don't like beer. There must be quite a few people who drink more than 153 liters! Here at the brewery we're allowed to drink as much beer as we want. As a result nobody drinks too much. At one time we had a limit of five beers a day, but then people felt they had to drink their "money's worth." Now that we don't have a limit, there are no problems.

The Faxe brewery has a fleet of trucks to deliver its beer to customers.

"We cultivate one million new trees a year"

Preben Møller is the State Forestry Superintendent for the Buderupholm district of the Rold Forest. The Rold Forest is the largest unbroken stretch of forest in Denmark, and is visited by thousands of people each year.

Here in Rold Forest we cultivate one million new trees a year. Some of these we plant out in our own forest and some we send out to other forest districts. About eleven per cent of the total area of the

One million trees are grown every year at this nursery in the Rold Forest.

country is covered by forest. Of this about five per cent is owned by the State. Rold Forest is the largest unbroken stretch of forest in Denmark and is about 8,000 hectares (20,000 acres) in size. About a third of this is owned by the State, and the rest is in private hands.

State forests are run on different lines from privately owned ones. We don't expect to make any money from the trees. We can take things other than profit into consideration. Danes prefer a tall, old beech forest, with a few oak and spruce dotted around and a forest floor covered with anemones. The beech is actually Denmark's national tree and in May, when the beech trees burst into leaf, Danes stream out into the forest to collect beech twigs to stand in a vase on their tables and mantlepieces.

Privately owned forests are expected to make money for the owners, of course. Mostly they are full of spruce trees. A spruce tree only takes about seventy years to reach the point where it can be cut down.

Beech trees may take anything up to 200 years. Denmark is at the northern limit of beech growing, so I suppose that's why they take so long to grow.

Most of the topsoil in Denmark is comparatively recent by geological standards, having been laid down by the glaciers that covered the country during the last Ice Age of around 12,000 years ago. During Stone Age times, most of Denmark was covered by oak forests, but these were largely cut down by herdsmen, farmers, woodcutters and charcoal burners. This deforestation became so bad that by 1800, forty per cent of Jutland had become relatively infertile heathland. Since then large areas of the country have been replanted. Now there are very few parts of Denmark that do not contain woods of some sort.

The Danish people love the outdoors. Jogging has become a national sport and we have a number of cross-country trails through Rold Forest. Orienteering races are also becoming more and more popular. Many clubs organize walks through the forest, and we arrange a Midsummer Eve festival at Lake Store Øxsø on June 23rd every year. In fact, we have more visitors than any other forest in Denmark. We have to make sure that they show consideration for the trees, of course, but we always have to remember that the State-owned forests are there for the benefit of the people. Fortunately, most people respect the rules of the forest, so we don't have too many problems to contend with.

Clearing up after fierce autumn storms that felled many trees in the forest.

"The landscape around here is so beautiful"

Poul Winther is an artist. He lives in Skagen, near the tip of Jutland, in a house which he built himself. Skagen is a popular place for artists and tourists. Besides painting, Poul does lithographs and sculptures.

I find my motifs and ideas on the beach. The beautiful things that get washed ashore have always fascinated me. I like to put them together to form interesting shapes and patterns.

Skagen means a lot to me. I've lived here all my life. Artists have been attracted to this area for a long time – the landscape is so beautiful. The quality of light is very bright because we have the sea on both sides of us. The sky seems to be so vast and the colors are so very clear.

It's rough here in winter because of the prevailing westerly wind, but for an artist roughness and bleakness have their charms too. The people here in north Jutland seem tougher than other Danes, probably because life up here has never been easy. The countryside used to be a

Poul at work on a new painting in the studio of the house he built himself.

The walls in Poul's house are decorated with examples of his works of art.

desolate landscape of sand dunes and bogs Now the bogs have been drained and turned into valuable farmland; spruce and fir trees act as a windbreak, and the wandering dunes have been brought under control by growing a tough grass to hold the sand in place. Before that the sand dunes used to drift and bury houses.

My parents wanted me to have some kind of education, so I became a carpenter's apprentice when I left school, and I thought of becoming an architect at one time. But I started painting and exhibiting my pictures while I was still an apprentice, so I never got that far. I had some of my paintings accepted for *Den Frie*, a well-known and respected exhibition in Copenhagen. After that I won an award to study painting in Paris.

Besides painting, I make lithographs and wood sculptures; I also design theater scenery and sometimes work with architects on the interior design of new buildings. Two years ago I spent a few months in Kuwait, on the Persian Gulf, working on the interior of a new hotel.

I find that working mostly at home means that I have to discipline myself to do some work every day. Of course it helps when you have a goal to work towards: completing a commission or preparing some new work for an exhibition. Many large firms and towns have their own arts funds. They use them to buy a number of original works each year for their collections which they circulate and exhibit in their buildings. The State also buys works to circulate around schools, and funds are available to enable museums to put on exhibitions. Danish artists are very pleased with these arrangements, because it means that not only do we sell something, but a lot of people get to see our work as well.

All this might make it sound as if being an artist is an easy living, but it isn't. It's become so difficult to sell paintings over the last couple of years that some artists have gone back to "ordinary" work and only paint in their spare time. Some are lucky enough to get a government grant for three years, and can devote all their time to their art. The old story about artists producing their best works when they are poverty-stricken isn't true. It's better not to have to worry where the next meal is coming from.

29

"School is compulsory for 9 years"

Tina Koldjær Jacobsen, 18, is in her final year at Hasseris high school in Ålborg. She is majoring in science and is thinking of becoming a nurse when she leaves.

I live in a village outside Ålborg, so I catch the school bus at 7:30 a.m. every day and come back on it at 3 p.m. When I get home at 3:30 p.m. I have a short rest and then, if I'm not helping out at the local post office for my pocket money, I get down to my homework. At the moment I've quite a bit of homework because exams are looming up. On average, I suppose I spend about two or three hours a day on review. Now I'm over 18, I get a government grant of just

Some of Tina's classmates have yet to arrive for this lesson in biology.

over 900 kroner ($90) a month.

In Denmark, school is compulsory for nine years, starting at the age of seven. After that you can either leave school, do another year at a comprehensive school that offers special technical, business or agricultural training, or continue in a sixth form college (a high school). More and more kids are continuing in sixth form, not only because the entrance requirements are getting so much harder for further education institutions, but also because it's better than being out of work.

There are four main "majors" in a sixth form college: science, languages, social subjects and music. Within each major you are allowed to choose a number of subjects. Which major you select depends on what you would like to do when you finish school.

Nearly all the schools that cover the nine compulsory years of education are run by the town councils. Each of these schools has a parent's board, which can have an influence on how the school's budget is spent and what teaching aids are used. The colleges – of which there are fewer – are usually run by the local country council or State. Because the Danes consider it important for everyone to have a choice in the education of their children, there are also some private schools, and so that everyone can afford the choice, these schools get 85 per cent subsidies from the government. Only about 7 per cent of schoolchildren go to these, though.

All this might sound pretty heavy, but I have time for fun as well. We have parties and enjoy ourselves, and in the last few years I've done a lot of horseback-riding in my spare time.

I'll be leaving school this summer and then I'll have to decide whether to carry on with my studies or get a job. I've been thinking of becoming a nurse. If I choose that as my career, I'll have to spend a year as mother's helper or work in a nursing home or something like that. Once that year's over, I'll have to try and get into nursing college. I just hope I'll be lucky, both in getting a job and then in getting to nursing college. It isn't easy these days and lots of applicants have to be turned away. I'm keeping my fingers crossed.

"Housing standards in Denmark are very high"

Jørgen Jørgensen is a member of the Social Democratic Party. He has been the Mayor of Køge for the last eight years. Køge is an important harbor for the importing of raw materials and the exporting of finished goods.

As Mayor, I preside over both political and administrative matters, that is to say, I'm head of the town council and of all the staff employed by it.

The town council of Køge consists of 21 elected members, representing various political parties. The Social Democrats are the largest in this borough – and the largest in the country.

Denmark is a constitutional monarchy: the powers of our sovereign are laid down

The Mayor of Køge at work in his office in the town hall.

in our Constitution. Unlike, say, the Queen of England, our monarchs are never crowned, but merely take over from the previous one. The current monarch, Queen Margrethe II, ascended the throne in 1972. She is Denmark's first queen since her namesake ruled in the fourteenth century.

Danish laws are made in our Parliament, the *Folketing*. This is made up of 179 members, with 2 members elected in Greenland and 2 in the Faroe Isles. Elections to the *Folketing* are by proportional representation. This means that the number of members of each party in Parliament is in proportion to the votes each party receives in the election: the more votes a party gets, the more members it has. The main parties at the moment are the Social Democrats, the Liberals, the Conservatives, and the Progressives. A delegate to the *Folketing* serves for four years. Every Dane over 18 has the right to vote in elections.

All laws enacted in the *Folketing* must

get the Queen's consent – usually a formality. They are then implemented by the government of the day. The government is headed by a prime minister, with a cabinet of ministers under him.

In 1970, our local government system was reorganized. The country was divided into 275 municipalities (led by elected municipal boards) and 14 counties (led by elected county councils). The municipalities are in charge of such matters as water, gas and electricity supplies, social welfare, primary schools, libraries and minor roads. The municipalities collect both income and property taxes, and receive grants from the government to help run their services. The county councils are responsible for such things as hospitals, secondary schools, main roads, and conservation of the countryside.

The municipalities have a large degree of self-government, but there are a number of laws from the county level and from central government which they have to administer. Our local government system is also democratic: every fourth year, people can elect whom they want to represent them.

The main task of any municipality, like the one I'm in charge of, is to spend the money it has sensibly, and without waste. Budgets must be drawn up – and kept to. This can often cause a lot of problems, because each party wants money to be used in different ways.

Here in Køge, we're concentrating on housing. We plan to build 400 new apartments every year. Even though the population of Køge and its surrounding areas isn't increasing appreciably, there is a pressing need for apartments for young people who want their own homes. Housing standards are very high. We figure on one room for each member of the family, plus one room for general use.

The Folketing, *Denmark's Parliament, has 179 members, each elected for four years.*

"My bearskin is about fifty years old"

A 'bearskin' is a military helmet made of fur. Arne Bækgård wears one when he stands guard. He is a soldier in the Royal Life Guards in Copenhagen. The main duty of the Guards is to protect the Queen and the other members of the Danish Royal Family. Arne is 20 years old.

The Guards are a special unit of the Danish Army – you have to volunteer for it but only 330 men are admitted every nine months. That's how long our conscription lasts. All men over the age of 18 have to report to the Draft Board, where they decide whether you're suitable for military service. My dad was a Life Guard too, so I'm following in his footsteps. Most of us come from Jutland and are sons of farmers, like me.

Discipline in the Guards is tough. As recruits we spent the first three months at a barracks in north Sjaelland. The training period finished with a really difficult test which we had to pass before we could join the unit. Then the first week was the hardest in my life. We were drilled and ordered around and marched up and down until we were ready to drop. But at least if you got through that you'd learned the parade drill, which you have to be able to do perfectly.

We stand guard outside the Amalienborg and Fredensborg Palaces, and we have orders not to let in anyone we don't know. Our rifles are always loaded with live ammunition, and if a person doesn't stop when we challenge them, we fire a warning shot into the air – after that we are supposed to shoot at them. I've never had to do that, and I can't remember anyone else having to, for that matter.

The bearskins we wear on duty get pretty hot, and if you don't choose one a few sizes bigger than your head, you may find yourself fainting. They don't make a new bearskin for every new recruit, and mine is about fifty years old.

Aside from draftees, there are other professional forces, such as the Territorial Army. This is a big, well-organized unit and it shares the same duties as the other armed forces. Everyone in the Territorials is a volunteer, and many of them used to serve in the regular army. There are quite a few women in the Territorials, as well as the other forces, but only on a voluntary basis. They receive exactly the same training as the men. I don't think there'll

ever be women in the Guards, however.

Denmark is a member of NATO (the North Atlantic Treaty Organization), which means that the size and the extent to which we modernize our forces is partly decided by the needs of NATO, rather than what's needed to defend Denmark. The other NATO countries have a say in the matter. Danish soldiers are also involved in United Nations Peace-keeping Forces in trouble spots such as Cyprus. Altogether we have approximately 34,000 people in the army, navy and air force, and a size-able number of planes, ships and equipment. But a resolution has been passed that no nuclear weapons will ever be permitted into Denmark during peacetime.

The Life Guards on parade in front of the Amalienborg Palace in Copenhagen.

If war ever did break out, it wouldn't be just a military problem; it would affect the civilian population just as much. For that reason we also have a large Civil Defense force to protect and help the civilian population during times of war. Civil Defense has always been well-supported since the German Occupation during the Second World War – it had about 70,000 members for many years, but this has slowly grown over the last ten years to around 73,000.

For the first three months, a new recruit under-goes rigorous training with the Guards.

"Danish clothes sell well abroad"

Leo Simonsen is 49 years old and a clothing manufacturer in Ikast. He started his own business eight years ago. Since then it has done better and better each year.

I employ thirty people in my factory — twenty-nine of them women of all ages, and one man. It's hard to find good sewing machine operators, so we also employ women to work at home. We provide them with a sewing machine and pay them a fixed rate for every garment they sew.

I've always worked in the clothing business. I started out on my own eight years ago, and I built this factory five years

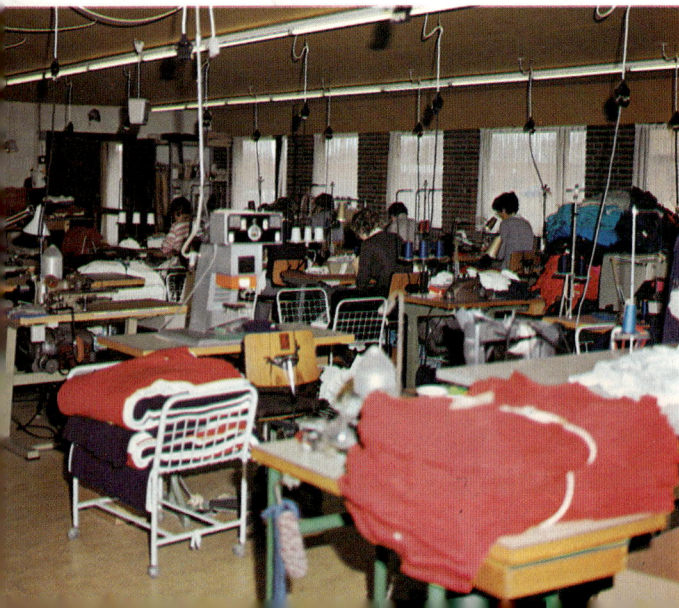

The sewing room of Leo's factory in Ikast. He also has women working at home for him.

ago because our sales had gone up so much, we needed to expand.

For many people it's hard work to set up on their own. It's quite common to start in a basement, sewing the clothes yourself and gradually build up the business. Denmark is famous for having numbers of small privately owned businesses with fewer than twenty employees. Unlike some other European countries, all manufacturing concerns in Denmark are privately owned, and there are no State subsidies. It's become more difficult to start out on your own — there are so many laws and regulations you have to comply with now, that many people are discouraged.

For me, though, it was surprisingly easy. I borrowed money from the bank, using my house as security. We had made sure of some orders from a few good customers, and after the first six months we were able to say we'd made a success of it. We were pretty lucky because the blouse we were producing at that time was a real "hit" on the market and sold very well indeed.

Three-quarters of our production is sold in Denmark; the rest goes to Norway and Sweden. We make blouse, dresses, skirts and casual clothing in knitted polyester and cotton fabrics. The blouses are our most successful line. Our market is based on just four big customers, who pay cash for their orders. That's good for us, because we don't need large credits at the bank – with the high interest rates on loans these days, you really have to try to steer clear of that. Having only a few customers means that we don't need sales representatives either, unlike most other clothing firms.

Our designers is also the head of our sewing room. When we make something new, the girls in the sewing room try it out. They are given a T-shirt or a dress and they just wear it normally for a while. Afterwards they tell us if there were any problems. That way we can correct any details before the garments are made in bulk.

To produce new designs you need inspiration, so once or twice a year my designer, my wife and I go down to Paris to look at clothes. That's still the place to go to find out what's new in the fashion world. We also take part in some of the international trade fairs that are arranged here in Denmark.

The area here around Ikast-Herning is a traditional textile and clothing region. The roots of the present industry go back hundreds of years, when the old moorland farmers produced handmade knitwear to supplement their poor incomes. Today, in Ikast alone, there are 180 clothing and textile factories. Some are bigger than others, of course. Danish clothes sell well abroad, because their quality is high and because they're well designed.

This shop sells casual clothing made at Leo's factory in Ikast.

"Denmark has many beautiful castles"

Bente Hatting Gjelten is 35 and a tourist guide in Copenhagen. She works at a tourist information center in a department store. She is currently writing a book on Hans Christian Andersen, the famous Danish fairy-tale writer.

I became a tourist guide by chance. I'd gained an MA (Master of Arts degree) in Drama, but afterwards I went to a school for guides because I wanted to learn some more useful, day-to-day English. English is Denmark's second language. At the end of the course I tried working as a guide for a while and I enjoyed it so much I stayed. That was seven years ago.

A few years ago, package vacations and group travel were quite the thing. Now

Bente works at the tourist information center in one of Copenhagen's large stores.

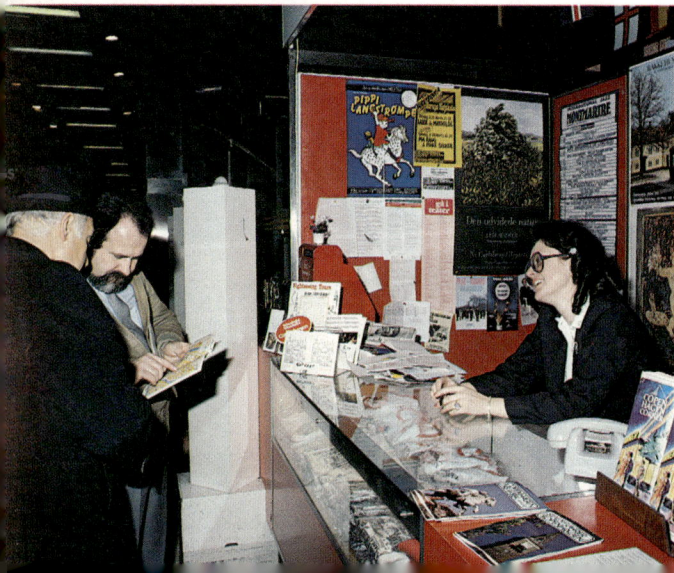

visitors tend to travel around on their own quite a lot, which means that the work of tourist information centers and guides has become even more important. Visitors need to know where things are, and where they can rent things, especially bicycles. There are literally millions of bicycles in Denmark, because the land is relatively flat. Cyclists are well-catered to, with cycle parks everywhere; and some buses even have a rack on the back to carry bikes. Many people rent a summer cottage and cycle around the countryside. The roads are mostly straight and there aren't that many cars on them. Once tourists used to come mostly in the summer, but now they also come in the winter to visit the theater or opera, and to hear the jazz. Copenhagen is now one of the best places for jazz in Europe. Then, of course, there's the Danish Royal Ballet and the many museums. These range from historical museums to art galleries – the modern art galleries also attract quite a lot of interest.

One of the most popular tours we offer is

into "Viking Country." The trip takes you through the Danish countryside, and we tell the tourists about our agricultural system and the Bronze Age barrows – the burial mounds built between 2000 and 500B.C. We visit the museum at Roskilde, which contains a number of Viking longships that were discovered accidentally in 1952 by frogmen investigating pollution in the fjord. We have a look, too, at Roskilde Cathedral, where the Danish monarchs are traditionally buried. The Cathedral is a landmark for miles around because of its beautiful tall green spires. We also drive down to Risø, the atomic research station, where Niels Bohr, the famous nuclear physicist, once worked. So the tour covers both ancient and modern Danish history.

Denmark has hundreds of beautiful castles and manor houses, nearly all of which are privately owned and still lived in. We called 1982 "Castle Year," because we managed to persuade quite a number of the "lords of the manor" to open their homes to tourists, including several castles that had never been open to the public before. One of the most beautiful is Frederiksborg Castle in Hillerød. It houses the Danish National Historical Museum – a massive collection of paintings, textiles and furniture. Its history can be traced back to 1560, but the castle you see today only goes back to the early 1600s, when it was rebuilt. Hans Christian Andersen described it as "rather Chinese" because of its bell-shaped towers.

The pride we take in our heritage is not just for the benefit of tourism. Danish people love anything old, and we carefully preserve castles, ancient monuments, and ordinary houses alike. Even in modern homes we seem to prefer old furniture.

In the summer, Copenhagen's Tivoli park is a popular place for both Danes and tourists.

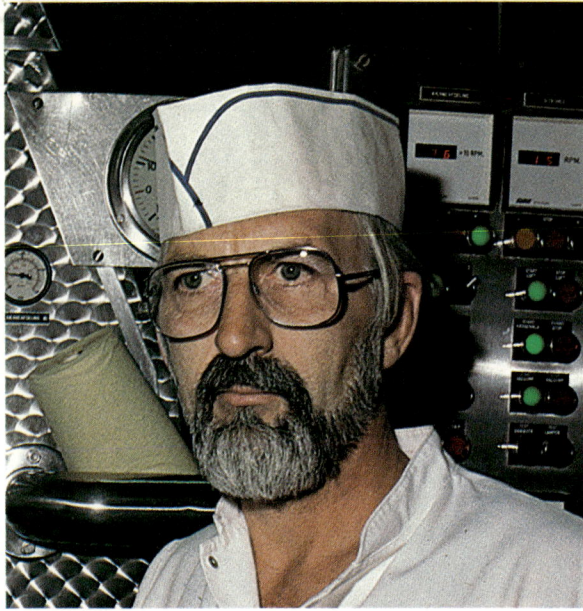

"Danes cannot do without their dairy products"

Frede Sørensen is a dairy worker at a butter-producing center in Hjørring. He has travelled to other parts of Scandinavia and to South America to advise on the setting up of dairies.

Our sole product here is butter. The cream comes in at one end of the dairy and butter comes out at the other end.

A modern Danish dairy is not, as it was in the old days, a place that produces lots of different dairy products. We have had to specialize. If you look at the small dairies that are left, those which have stuck to a mixed production are in difficulty, because everything these days requires specialization and mechanization.

We get our cream from half a dozen dairies dotted around north Jutland – and from the Denmark Dairy, which is next door to us.

The cream starts to arrive round about noon – in tank trucks or through pipes from the dairy next door. We weigh it out, pasteurize it at 108°C (226°F) and cool it down again to 4°C (39°). After that, it is transferred to the tanks around the churn.

At the dairy, Frede operates the churn that turns the cream into butter.

Much of the cream for the butter arrives at the dairy in tank trucks like this one.

There half of the cream is turned sour. It's the dairyman's job to ensure that we get the right proportion of sour and "sweet" cream.

I regulate the process by means of a panel of buttons next to the churn. The churning is a continuous process; that is to say the cream goes in at one end of the churn and the butter comes out at the other end. The churn is turning all the time. I control the process so that the quantity of finished butter corresponds to the packing capacity available.

Every day we have 77 tons of cream coming in, from which we produce 35 tons of butter. All the butter we produce here is for export, but of course there are other dairies which produce butter for the home market. Altogether about 70 per cent of the butter produced in Denmark is for foreign markets.

During the churning process the cream is kept at a temperature of 11° to 12°C (52° to 54 °F) to get it to churn into butter. There is also a by-product from this process – buttermilk – which is sent to another dairy for packaging to be sold here in Denmark.

Because the technical side of the dairy industry has advanced enormously, the number of people being employed in it has been growing smaller and smaller.

The milk comes from our dairy cattle, of which there are 1.25 million in Denmark – a great number of them here in Jutland. We have various breeds: the ones that give the most milk are the Black-and-White Danish breed (45 per cent of the total number of cattle); Jersey cows give the milk with the greatest fat content (18 per cent); and the Red Danish dairy breed is also a good milker (29 per cent).

We have over twenty different kinds of milk products, not counting all the different kinds of cheeses. Danes cannot do without their dairy products. We use a lot of cream in cooking, even whipped cream in soups. In recent years curd products, such as junket and yogurt, have become extremely popular. Many children have one or the other for breakfast.

Denmark is famous both for its dairy products and for its dairy machinery. I have just been to Venezuela, where I helped start up a new butter-producing dairy. I was there for a month. That's not very long, but I managed to teach them the basics and adjust the churn to suit their production requirements.

"Six yards have had to close"

John Jensen is 43. He works as a fitter, making parts for ships' diesel engines, at the shipyard in Elsinore (Helsingør in Danish). John is also a shop steward for the millers and turners in the Metal Workers' Union.

We Danes have always been a seafaring people, so it's not surprising that shipbuilding is one of our major industries. Shipbuilding, like most Danish industries, is a "processing" one: raw materials are imported, assembled, and then exported. Because we have no raw materials of our own, everything for our manufacturing industry has to be brought in from abroad. This means that we must export a lot of our products to pay for the high import bills.

At the moment we're building some really beautiful luxury liners for Iraq — we've got four under construction actually. We also repair ships. Many of the shipyards in Denmark are going through a rough patch at the moment because of the worldwide slump in shipping. Six yards have had to close, and the number of new vessels on order is at its lowest since the mid-1950s. Fortunately, we seem to be managing all right and the future is quite bright. We're expecting some orders from the Soviet Union soon. It would be a real feather in our cap if we got them.

I'm a shop steward for the millers and turners — the men who use the machines that shape the metal to make the parts for the engines. I represent about fifty men in the "shop" (department of the factory where all the workers belong to one trade union). As a shop steward, I am the person

The Elsinore shipyard is currently building four luxury liners for Iraq.

who has to negotiate with the management about wages and working conditions. We've just had some pay talks and we managed to get a small raise in wages. But we had to have three rounds of discussions before both sides could come to an agreement on the size of the increase.

We're quite peaceful in this shop — perhaps it's because we've all been here a long time. Most of the men in this department have been at this shipyard for around twenty-five years, so we're more easygoing than the youngsters. Compared to other European countries, Denmark loses fewer working days because of labor disputes. But I think that the modern generation of workers seems more aggressive than us older men, and they demand too much. We don't mind getting low pay raises because we want to keep our jobs. But the cost of living today is much higher than it was when I was young: housing and transportation, for example, were much cheaper then.

Quite a few of the older workers here are opting for early retirement. They stop working at 60, and initially get 90 per cent of their wages and a small State pension. In the years between retiring and reaching the normal retirement age of 67, the percentage of their last wages gets smaller, while the level of pension rises, until they get a full State old-age pension when they reach 67.

It's a good arrangement, because people can have time to enjoy themselves before they get too old, and younger people can take over their jobs. In these times of high unemployment, it's good to get some of the youngsters working, so they don't just sit around twiddling their thumbs all day.

The workshop at the shipyard, where John makes parts for ships' diesel engines.

"Our potted plants are sold all around Europe"

Niels Pedersen is 33 and a nursery gardener at Lumby, near Odense. He and his two brothers run the business, which was started by their father. Since taking over the nursery, they have doubled its size and introduced many energy-saving processes.

The island of Fyn is known as the "Garden of Denmark" and we have a long tradition of plant and tree nurseries and fruit growing here. My two brothers and I are relative newcomers to running a business. We took over our father's nursery four years ago. At that time we had 3,000 square meters (32,000 square feet) of greenhouses.

Today we've got 6,000 square meters (64,500 square feet) under glass, half of which have been specially constructed as "low-energy" greenhouses, that is to say they're made of double acrylic sheeting and have shades to prevent the heat from escaping in the evening.

Today the vital thing for gardeners producing hothouse plants is to keep their energy consumption down – if they want to survive as gardeners, that is! And with our production of potted plants, we have to have a high temperature in the greenhouses all through the year.

Our biggest sales are ferns, which we grow all the year long. We get the young plants from Holland. While they're growing we have to ensure that they have the best possible conditions. We've done this by making everything as efficient and mechanized as possible: temperature and humidity are regulated automatically; the plants are kept watered by channels in the shelves – the water contains all the fertilizers that they need.

Another, more specialized item we deal in is banana plants. We've only been growing them for a couple of years. We get them as tiny plants from Israel. It takes six months for our banana plants to grow big enough to be sold. And the market for them is getting bigger and bigger. We also have to think to the future, so we're continually experimenting with new plants – you never know how long it will be before people decide they don't want to buy banana plants anymore.

The fact that we've been able to survive as gardeners is due to our excellent sales setup. In Denmark we have an organization of professional gardeners, known as

GASA, which looks after our sales for us. It's a cooperative association owned by the members, and it works really well. Its sales activities are concentrated mainly on overseas markets. Our potted plants are sold all around Europe, as far south as Greece and Turkey, and as far north as Greenland (which is part of Denmark) and the other countries of Scandinavia. Our biggest customer is West Germany.

In our opinion the gardening business is one of the most flexible and unpredictable in the country. We have to be ready for changes the whole time if we want to

One of the large, "low-energy" greenhouses on the nursery which Niels helps to run.

Tulips are also grown at the nursery, but not under glass.

survive, and we have to make the changes quickly. When the energy crisis hit us in 1976, we suddenly found ourselves having to pay twice as much for oil – without being able to put the prices for our products up to the same extent. That meant there was only one way to survive: to cut down on our overhead. Hence all the energy-saving measures. The situation today is that plant prices have dropped, so our profit per plant is lower than last year. In other words, we now have to find a way to grow our plants more efficiently to get the same profit.

"Greenland is the world's largest island"

Nukakuluk Kreutzmann, 27, was born and bred in Greenland. Although 3,000 km (2,000 miles) away, it is part of Denmark. Nukakuluk is training to be a social worker in Copenhagen.

Greenland is my home and I'm looking forward to going back there. There are very few opportunities for higher education in Greenland, so eight years ago I came to Denmark to go to a technical college. At the moment there are about 1,000 Greenlanders living over here.

I'm now married to a Dane, whom I met in Greenland. Luckily he likes Greenland as much as I do. So the first opportunity we

Icebergs are a constant hazard to the fishermen of Greenland's ports.

get, we'll be moving back up there. One of the biggest problems in moving is living quarters. Being so far north, building work in Greenland is only possible during a few months in the summer. Consequently, there is a shortage of houses.

Greenland is a completely different country from Denmark. The landscape is so beautiful and so vast – it's about fifty times larger than Denmark, and the world's largest island. I miss its huge, peaceful open spaces. Some 50,000 people live there, 10,000 of whom are Danes. In the last thirty years, Greenland has modernized rapidly and social standards have improved enormously. Now there is better housing, better hygiene and higher wages.

Greenland exports such things as cod, salmon, lamb, furs, lead and zinc. And there are enormous underground deposits of iron ore, uranium and other valuable minerals which have yet to be mined.

In 1979 Greenland held a referendum on home rule. This showed that most Greenlanders wanted to be more independent

Most of Greenland is covered with ice and snow throughout the year.

of Denmark and decide things for themselves. Now our Parliament, the *Landsting*, in Godthab (Greenland's capital) decides how Greenland should be run. The Danish Parliament, where there are two representatives from Greenland, still handles defense policy and foreign affairs. So we haven't lost all contact with Denmark. She still gives us about one billion kroner ($100 million) annually.

Life in Greenland has changed a lot in thirty years. The Danes wanted to make it a place where people lived like Danes and behaved like Danes. I'm sure that they meant well, but when you've been a hunter in the wilds all your life, it's difficult to adapt suddenly to a more civilized world. And it really has given many Greenlanders a lot of problems. There is still a high level of unemployment among young Greenlanders, and alcoholism has increased greatly. We all hope that home rule will help to put these things right again.

My job as a social worker at the Danish Office for Home Rule in Copenhagen is to keep in touch with hospital patients from Greenland. If you are seriously ill, they can't deal with it in Greenland so they have to fly the patients down to the hospital here in Copenhagen. But these people may have many unsolved problems: What happens when they're well again? What about their children while they're down here? And so on. I try to help them with these problems.

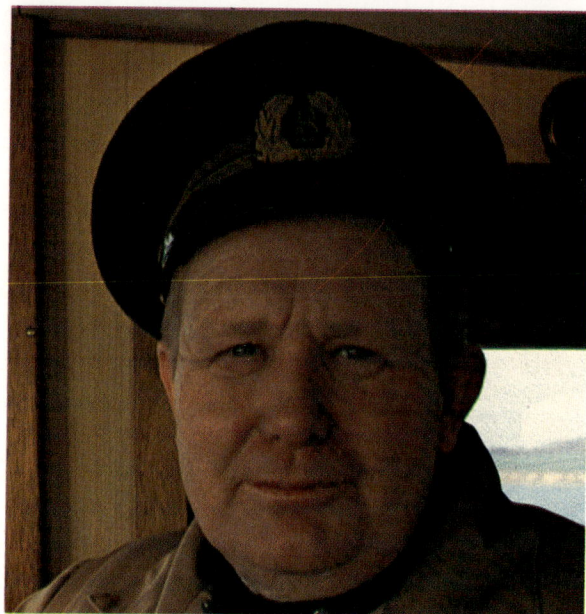

"Denmark is an island community"

Knud Erik Pedersen is 46, and has been operating the ferry between Assens and the island of Baagø for the last twenty years. During this time Knud has seen the population of the island decrease year by year as people move to the mainland.

Life on the islands isn't easy these days, and people are leaving them, especially the smaller ones. Today, Baagø has 63 inhabitants; twenty years ago it had 210.

There are seven children on Baagø who use the ferry every day to go to school in Assens, on the mainland. When they leave school, I doubt if they will settle on the island. There isn't anything for them to do on Baagø, except farming – and that's not exactly profitable.

I've sailed back and forth between Assens and Baagø for twenty years. For the first nine years I owned my own ferry, which I sailed every day. Then the route was taken over by the district and county council, the island's inhabitants and the Post Office. So now I'm employed by them as a captain on this route.

In the days when I owned the route myself, I was on my own and never had a day off in five years. But I seemed to manage. Now it's a much easier job, and I have plenty of free time. We go camping a bit, my wife and I, and folk dancing; but apart from that I don't have many interests.

I suppose that's because there was never time for that kind of thing before.

We live in Assens which is a little town in Fyn. As a child I lived on Mors, which is an island in Lii Fjord. My wife is from Bornholm, an island in the Baltic. So we are really islanders. People usually say the islanders are a special breed, that they don't do much socializing. I think that's true. At any rate, we get on well only having a few friends. In fact we like being on our own. Denmark is an island community. There are 406 islands of varying size.

It can be a bit of a problem in winter getting round to the islands and across to the mainland. Many of the connections between the islands are cut off by the ice that builds up between them. The crossing between Assens and Baagø is the only one open every day, right through the winter. So the people on Baagø don't have to go without their provisions. During the worst periods in winter, though, we can only make one trip out there and back. Normally we make four trips in each direction. It takes half an hour each way.

There is a big difference between summer and winter here. 'Round about Easter time, the tourists start to arrive. People go camping or to the summer cottages over on the island: the population more than doubles during the summer season.

In spring, I ferry seed corn and artificial fertilizers across to the island's farmers. In late summer, the harvesting starts and we ferry the corn back to Assens. In the autumn, we bring over the sugar beets grown on the island, to the sugar refinery in Assens.

Being a ferryman is anything but boring. You get to know all the local people, chat with them and keep in touch with what's going on. If the islanders are going to a party after my normal sailing times, they have to phone me and get me to ferry them across. That costs a bit extra, but there's always someone on duty. After all you are pretty isolated living on an island.

Knud at the controls of the Assens to Baagø ferry. He has been a ferryman for 20 years.

Today, only 63 people live on Baagø. Knud keeps them in contact with the mainland.

"People are fed up with the dull bread from supermarkets"

Kjeld Beck, 36, works in a bakery at the shopping center in Farum, a suburb of Copenhagen. He has been in the business for the past twenty-two years. He finds that people are now more fussy about the bread they buy.

I just have to put the icing on this strip of Danish pastry. I take the piece of paper and make it into a cone. Then I fill the cone with icing and snip off the end. And one, two, three, there's the pastry iced! It's funny that other nationalities call these Danish pastries and we know it as Vienna bread.

Our shop opens every day at 7 a.m., so to get everything ready we start work at 2:30 in the morning. Parliament once tried to introduce a law to stop bakers' working before 6 a.m. and to close the bakeries on Sundays, but the law was never passed. I think even the politicians are too used to buying their bread and cakes on Sundays! We continue to bake until 10:30 a.m. and

Kjeld prepares the icing for some freshly baked Danish pastries for the bread shop.

The bakery is at the rear of the bread shop in Farum's shopping center.

then we are free. Usually I'll go home to bed until 5 p.m., spend the evening with my family and then go back to bed when they do. I've been a baker for twenty-two years, so my family has got used to these strange hours.

In recent years we've started baking lots of different types of coarse bread, that is to say wholemeal breads with different types of seeds or grain. We make walnut bread, bread with sunflower seeds, "4-in-1" with four different kinds of corn, and the dark rye bread that is usually used in making *smørrebrød* – the famous Danish open sandwich that can have a infinite variety of toppings. One restaurant has a *smørrebrød* list one meter (39 inches) long! The bread has a higher fat content than in other countries. It means the bread keeps fresh longer, but there are more calories in it. Of course our famous cream-filled pastries are

very fattening too, and people certainly don't buy as many of the big cream cakes now as they used to. It might be the cost, but I think it's because people are thinking more about their health.

We have a modern bakery here, with two ovens that can each bake 700 loaves. We also have machines that can mix the dough, roll it out and weigh it, so that each loaf is the same weight. All the same, most of the work is done by hand as this produces a better consistency.

As with all shops selling foodstuffs, we get regular visits from the Public Health Inspector, who checks that the standard of hygiene in the shop and bakery is maintained, and also that the ingredients we use are of good quality.

"There was snow inside the locomotive"

Poul Busk, 62, is a locomotive engineer on the DSB, the Danish State railroad. He has been working on the railroad for over thirty years, and has seen steam engines replaced by more modern diesel-electric locomotives.

When I first started here, back in 1948, we still had steam trains. I started as a fireman, and I was the one who had to grease all the valves and connecting rods on the locomotive. At that time you had to say "Mister" to your engine driver: there was one door on the locomotive for the fireman

The Danish State railroad has just taken delivery of the MZ series of locomotive.

and one for the engine driver, and Heaven help the fireman who got in through the wrong door!

Times have changed. These days you sit back in a comfortable seat and skim along the tracks. You're quite alone on most of the routes. For that reason, we have a radio in the cabin, so you can call someone up in an emergency. It's a more boring job now, because contact with other people is important, especially on a long journey.

We've just received some brand-new locomotives from Germany – the MZ series. We're running them in on the express route from Copenhagen to Arhus. They'll cut down the traveling time between the two cities. That's the important thing today – cutting down traveling time, making the distances between the various parts of the country shorter.

A lot of people still use their own car to get to and from work, but gas is very expensive these days, so more and more people are taking the bus or train instead. And a lot of people also cycle to work.

The cab of a modern locomotive – cleaner and more comfortable than a steam engine's.

Bikes have really come into their own again since gasoline prices started to go up. Cycle shops are doing a roaring trade and the exercise people get from cycling does them good. People have also started using their bikes on vacation, cycling from one youth hostel to another.

In the Greater Copenhagen area the "S-trains" – the suburban electric trains – are the main means of transportation. The driver has to whistle when the train is leaving the station, close the doors and then drive the train. Because he is all on his own, there is a "dead-man's handle" connected to the speed control. If the control is not in use for a period of more than two and a half seconds, the emergency system comes into operation and the train grinds to a halt automatically.

Sometimes things happen that you could well do without. A few years ago, for example, a train got stuck in a snowdrift. There was snow up to the windows and inside the locomotive. The driver couldn't do a thing except sit and wait – and he was absolutely freezing. Suddenly he saw a man with a long, white beard right in front of his window, and he thought he had gone crazy. But it turned out it was just a farmer living nearby who wanted to help. The driver stayed at the farmer's house for four days before a helicopter came to pick him up. Because there was so much snow, no vehicle could get through.

53

"It isn't easy being an artist today"

Jette Nevers is 37 years old, and a textile artist. She lives in an old schoolhouse in Hasmark, Fyn island, with her husband, who's a blacksmith, and her three children.

I suppose it took eleven years before I really made my breakthrough. I finished my studies at the Copenhagen School of Arts and Crafts in 1965, and it was only in 1976 that I had some of my work accepted for the Charlottenborg exhibition. This exhibition is very important for Danish artists, because that's where you become known and recognized as an artist.

Not only did I have three of my works accepted, they were also sold – to the New Carlsberg Foundation and two art societies.

In the same year I had a one-woman show at the Museum of Applied Art. And that too was a success. I sold everything and got glowing reviews in the papers. That's what gave me the push to really start selling my work.

I weave tapestries, carpets, altarpieces and various decorations for public institutions. My husband Henrik has built me an electric spinning wheel where I can spin the yarn for my tapestries.

My workshop is on the first floor of the school. There I have my looms, wool and sketches for my next projects. There are three of us in the workshop – myself and two pupils. They're usually girls from abroad, who get board, lodgings and pocket money, plus the materials for everything they want to weave. In normal working hours, they weave for me; after that they can weave for themselves – as much as they want.

It's good for me having them here. They keep me on my toes, because passing on knowledge and keeping up-to-date in your field is very important. And it's up to the girls themselves to decide whether they want to become artists or weavers. I can only give them an introduction to the art of weaving. They have to go to the School of Arts and Crafts in Copenhagen or Kolding for their formal education.

At the moment I'm working on a number of things for churches. I've been doing sketches and drawings for altar hangings and kneelers. I take a lot of trouble over all the sketches and samples, which have to be

54

Jette at work on her loom in the workshop on the first floor of the schoolhouse.

judged by the parish and town councils, as well as architects, because I know how much workmanship and finish mean in a case like this. Apart from being an artist, I'm also a craftsman – or woman! It's no use making things for their artistic appeal if they aren't made well. That's probably also one of the secrets of my success, if you want to call it that. Since the age of the Vikings, Danish craftsmen have been renowned for the design of their products. Danish furniture, for example, has influenced designers all over the world.

It isn't easy being an artist today. Many artists can't earn enough to make ends meet. That's not because they're bad artists; there may be lots of other reasons. For example, I know a sculptor who is very good, the only trouble is he's very slow and meticulous. Because of the time he takes, his pieces are expensive and few people can afford them. Most artists choose to make their art a sideline and have a regular job, as well – but that's not a very good idea, in my opinion.

Jette has just finished weaving this wall-hanging for one of her customers.

"The degree of violence used is getting worse"

Police Inspector K. Larsen, 36, is a member of the Danish Police Force in Elsinore. Trained as a car mechanic, he left his trade when it went into a recession to join the police.

To get into the police force you have to be at least 1.77 meters (5ft 8in) tall, be good at Danish – so that you can express yourself clearly and write reports – have a completely clean record, of course, and be in good physical shape.

I joined the force relatively late. I was a car mechanic originally, but that trade is in a recession at the moment, so my wife and I agreed that I'd have to find another, more steady job somewhere else.

Elsinore harbor is one of the areas Inspector Larsen patrols on his daily beat.

And there's plenty to do here in Elsinore. It's not exactly what you'd call a peaceful neck of the woods – because of the short ferry crossing to Sweden. Not that Swedes are particular troublemakers, it's just that they have stricter licensing laws over alcohol in Sweden than in Denmark, and a lot of Swedes take advantage of the fact. They come over here in droves on Saturday evening and then we have to spend most of Sunday getting them back on the ferry. In general, the rule for drunks is that we put them in a cell for the night and let them out again the next day. We don't write a report and we don't prosecute.

I belong to the uniformed branch, which is the largest section of the force. We take care of all the day-to-day cases, while the more complicated cases are handed over to the detective branch for investigation. We deal with such things as demonstrations, vandalism, brawls, regulation of traffic and so on.

Luckily it's not every day we have to deal with violent cases. Over the last two years, however, there has been a rise in crimes of robbery and violence. And it isn't just the number of cases that is on the increase: the degree of violence used is getting worse and more horrible. It has become more common for people to carry illegal guns or long knives. And, what's more, they're not afraid to use them.

As serious crimes are getting worse, the penalties for less serious offenses are getting weaker. That means you have to do something really bad before you get a severe punishment. The legal system is overburdened, so it may take quite a long time from when a person is sentenced until they actually go to prison. That seems rather unfortunate in the case of a violent criminal, but that's the way it is.

Here in Denmark we have a number of open prisons where inmates are allowed to go home on weekends. We hope that these types of prisons will have a more preventive and constructive effect than the old type of prison. Criminals convicted of more serious crimes are, of course, still kept in closed prisons with tight security, but for less-serious offenses there is this more open form of captivity. We hope that a lot of youngsters may be able to get out of their criminal environment if we treat them a little better than they do in the old-fashioned prisons. They can also study and work in the open prisons.

One of the duties of the Danish police force is to control demonstrations, like this one.

"We were the first country to start a soccer team"

Kenneth Christiansen is 14 years old and in the ninth grade. He plays soccer and tennis in his spare time. Soccer is one of Denmark's national sports.

I go training twice a week, and we have a match once a week. Last year we won the Sjaelland Championship. The team was very proud. We were in the newspapers several times and we got a cup. Soccer is a national sport here. In fact, we were the first country to start a soccer team —

There's usually enough snow in winter for skiing, but Kenneth prefers soccer.

way back in 1873.

Even though it's fun and exciting playing soccer, I'm not thinking of becoming a professional player. I play soccer because I enjoy it, and not because I want to earn a living from it. Professional soccer was only introduced in Denmark in 1978. It was hoped that this would keep all our best players from leaving the country to earn a living playing with teams in other European countries and in America. The change to professional soccer has not been very successful, because managers are not used to running their teams along business lines.

In the first year, at least one team went bankrupt and most of the others had financial problems. And the players found that they were earning the same amount of money as they had been when they were playing part-time. Part of the problem was that the standard of soccer did not improve and not enough people went to matches to provide the teams with an income. There just aren't enough people in

Kenneth plays a lot of soccer, but does not want to become a professional.

Denmark to support the thirty-six teams in our three divisions.

I also play tennis once a week during the summer. It's not too expensive then, but in winter, when you have to play on indoor courts, it costs 140 kroner ($14) a month – and that's more than I can afford. Normally, all the sports activities get money from the local council. Instructors, soccer fields and tennis courts all cost money, and if we had to pay for them ourselves, few people could afford it.

In my class, almost everyone does some kind of sport in their spare time. In winter we have quite a lot of snow and the lakes get frozen over. So many people go skiing and skating.

Jogging has also become very popular in Denmark in the last few years. Many people, especially businessmen, go out every morning before they go off to sit behind their desks. I think it's because doctors are now saying that if you don't get enough exercise, you're more likely to get blood clots or something. So you have to keep fit and keep in shape. A lot of grown-ups seem to have realized this. Now it's common to see people running in the woods or along roads and paths.

A lot of local councils have also built swimming pools, where it's very cheap to go for a swim or to take swimming lessons. Here in Denmark it's very important to be able to swim, because there's so much water around us. Badminton and cycling are also very popular sports here, too, but soccer will always be my favorite!

"More and more people are going to the theater"

Finn Rye Petersen, 35, is an actor and cofounder of the Boat Theater, a converted river barge which is permanently moored in Nyhavn, a suburb of Copenhagen. He also teaches at the State School of Drama.

I suppose I'm what you'd call a self-taught actor. I've always wanted to be an actor, and began appearing in plays at school. But I never went on to study at one of the three theatrical schools in Denmark. In fact, I'm a qualified electronics draftsman, although I've never used it for any

The barge is not as comfortable as most theaters but it is usually a packed house.

purpose. Now I teach basic acrobatics and mime at the State School of Drama in Copenhagen.

As a nation we've always considered the theater an important part of our cultural heritage. This is reflected in the number of theaters in such a small country. There are 15 in Copenhagen, 10 in the provinces – in such cities as Arhus, Odense and Aalborg – and some 40 traveling theaters.

Our theater season runs from September to June. There are no performances during the summer months, except for special shows for vacationers and at the Pantomime Theater in Copenhagen's famous Tivoli Gardens — its open-air stage, with acrobats and clowns, and firework displays on weekends, always attract a large audience. Also, a troupe of English actors comes over every summer to perform *Hamlet* in Kronberg Castle, in Elsinore, where William Shakespeare originally set his play.

Copenhagen's Royal Theater is the country's largest. It has about sixty productions a year – plays, ballets and operas. It has 45 resident actors, 90 dancers, an opera chorus of 61 and an orchestra of 100 musicians. So it's not surprising that is costs about 110 million kroner ($11 million) a year to run. The theater earns about 10 million kroner; the rest is made up with a subsidy from the State. The State support given to the Royal Theater is almost twice as much as the payments it gives to the rest of our theaters: the other Copenhagen theaters get about 70 million kroner a year, and the traveling theaters about 15 million kroner.

The Boat Theater started life in 1972, when we bought an old river barge. "We" were a mixed bunch of people, from a variety of backgrounds and occupations. It took quite a long time to convert the barge into a theater, so our first performance wasn't until 1973 – and it was a success. We like to think of ourselves as a family theater, because many of our productions are for both adults and children. Now that we are established, we receive a large grant from the Ministry of Cultural Affairs.

Theaters starting up nowadays have to survive initially on their box office returns. Consequently, many of the smaller theaters have difficulty keeping their heads above water and paying their actors a decent wage. Some of them quickly disappear, but new ones are always popping up to replace them.

Denmark has a nationwide organization which sells theater tickets at a discount price, provided you agree to see a certain number of plays a year. This helps us a lot, because the organization distributes publicity material about plays to every home in Denmark. This has encouraged more and more people to go to the theater, which must be a good thing.

The Boat Theater was formed over ten years ago and is now permanently based in Nyhavn.

Facts

Capital city: Copenhagen (København).

Principal language: Danish. Faroese is spoken on the Faroe Islands and Eskimo in Greenland, although Danish is compulsory in these islands' schools

Currency: 100 ore = 1 Danish krone = 10 US cents.

Religion: 94% of the population belong to the Danish Lutheran Church, which is the established church. There are small communities of Roman Catholics, Jews and Baptists.

Population: 5.12 million (1980). 25% live in and around Copenhagen. Denmark is comparatively densely populated. The population is almost entirely Scandinavian. In 1976 97% of Denmark's inhabitants had been born in Denmark, including the Faroe Islands and Greenland.

Climate: Temperate. Mild summers and cold, rainy winters. The weather is changeable.

Government: Constitutional monarchy. The reigning monarch is Queen Margrethe II, who ascended the throne in 1972. Every other Monday the Queen holds an audience for any citizen with a reasonable request. In principle she has all the executive power, but exercises it through her prime minister and cabinet. There is a single-chamber Parliament – the *Folketing*. It has 179 members, with 2 members representing the Faroe Islands and 2 members Greenland. In 1980 there were 42 women members. Members are elected for 4 years by proportional representation. Voting is not compulsory, and is open to all men and women over the age of 18, including prison inmates. The Faroe Islands and Greenland are self-governing regions. Foreign affairs, defense and some other matters are decided by the *Folketing*, while internal matters have been devolved to their own Parliaments, the *Lagting* (Faroes) and *Landsting* (Greenland). The main political parties are the Social Democrats, the Liberals, the Conservatives, and the Progressive Party.

Local Government: In a major reform in 1970, the country was divided up into 275 municipalities *(Kommuner)*, each led by an elected board, and 14 counties *(Amtskommuner)*, each headed by elected councils. The municipalities are responsible for water, gas and electricity supplies, plus social welfare, primary schools, libraries, and local roads. County Councils administer hospital services, higher schools, main roads, theaters, extraction of raw materials, and nature conservation. The municipalities collect both income and property taxes, and receive large grants from the government.

Housing: More than 40% of the population live in their own homes, the majority of which are in high-rise buildings. 30% of these buildings have been built since 1960. 55% of all housing is for single families. The average size of homes is one of the largest in Europe.

Education: 90% of children attend State schools – called *Folkeskolen* (People's school). The remaining 10% go to private schools or have home instruction. Most children go to a kindergarten, at the age of 5 or 6, before undertaking 9 years of compulsory education. After the ninth (or optional tenth) year, about 35% of school pupils choose a 2 or 3 year general literary or mathematical course which can lead to further education at university or other higher level center. About 30% choose a 2½ to 4 year vocational training course in crafts, industry, office or commerce. The remainder continue with different forms of preparatory training or seek work where training is provided. Denmark has been described as the country with the largest and most varied range of choices in youth education. Denmark has 5 universities and 3 technical universities. Adults can continue their education at the 90 folk high schools and by attending night school.

Agriculture: In 1979 this accounted for 20% of Denmark's exports. The main exports are: butter, beef and bacon. Pigs outnumber people by 2 to 1! Agriculture is organized on a co-operative basis. Farmers and small landowners form co-op societies,

Glossary

which market the produce and carry out research. About 70% of the country is used for agriculture, and it is intensively farmed. More than 50% of the cultivated land is devoted to cereals. Dairy farming is also important.

Industry: Industry accounts for over 67% of Denmark's exports. Most firms are small and privately owned. The emphasis is on light rather than heavy manufacturing. Since Denmark has few raw materials, much has to be imported. Important industries are: food processing, beverages, cement, shipbuilding, engineering, chemicals, furniture, electronics, porcelain, and textiles. 77% of all employees are members of trade unions.

The Media: *Danmarks Radio* has the monopoly of radio and television broadcasting. It is publicly owned but independently run by a council of 27 members, chosen by the *Folketing*, headed by a Director General. Neither television nor radio carry advertisements, being financed by license payments alone. There are over 220 newspapers some 48 of which are dailies. The circulation of newspapers per head is one of the highest in the world. Most of the papers are no longer connected with a political party.

Barrow Earth heaped over one or more graves.

Bearskin A tall helmet, covered with fur, worn by soldiers, usually only for ceremonial purposes.

Bronze Age The period between the Stone and Iron Ages (4500 to 500 B.C.) during which weapons and tools were made of bronze.

Common Market see **EEC**

Dead man's handle A safety switch on a piece of machinery, such as a trian, that allows the machine to function only while depressed by the operator.

EEC European Economic Community, or Common Market. An association of nations, created chiefly to promote free trade among member nations and to adopt common import duties on goods from other countries.

Home Rule The desire of states which are part of a nation to become more independent and to manage their own affairs.

Ice Age The period in history when much of the earth's surface was covered by ice.

Iron Age The period after the Bronze Age, during which there was a rapid spread of iron tools and weapons.

Licensing laws The rules governing the sale of an item – alcohol, for example.

Missionary A member of a church who goes to a country to convert people to his own faith.

NATO An international organization, composed of the United States, Canada, Iceland, Britain and 11 other European countries, including Denmark.

Open prison A prison where there is less security and more freedom for prisoners.

Pasteurize The process of heating liquids and solids to destroy harmful germs.

Recession A temporary slackening off of business activity.

Slaughterhouse A place where animals are killed to supply us with food.

Stone Age A period in history when humans used tools and weapons made out to stone.

Index